The GIRLS' Book 3

EVEN **MORE** WAYS TO BE THE
BEST AT EVERYTHING

Written by Tracey Turner
Illustrated by Katy Jackson
Edited by Philippa Wingate
Designed by Zoe Quayle

The GIRLS' Book 3

Book

EVEN MORE WAYS TO BE THE BEST AT EVERYTHING

Buster Books

First published in Great Britain in 2009 by Buster Books,
an imprint of Michael O'Mara Books Limited,
9 Lion Yard, Tremadoc Road, London SW4 7NQ

www.mombooks.com/busterbooks

For Sophie and Lucy Dinning

A CIP catalogue record for this book is available from the British Library.

ISBN: 978-1-906082-76-5

2 4 6 8 10 9 7 5 3 1

Printed and bound in England by Clays Ltd, St Ives plc

Papers used by Michael O'Mara Books are natural, recyclable products
made from wood grown in sustainable forests. The manufacturing processes
conform to the environmental regulations of the country of origin.

NOTE TO READERS

CONTENTS

How To Flip A Pancake 8

How To Work Out Your Dog's 'Human Age' 10

How To Make Your Own Christmas Crackers 11

How To Play The Name Game 14

How To Remember The Planets In The Solar System 15

How To Make Spaghetti Jellyfish 16

How To Confuse Your Brain And Body 17

How To Hide Your Secret Papers 18

How To Make Amazing Muesli 19

How To Perform The Heimlich Manoeuvre 20

How To Tell Which Way Is North 21

How To Speak 'Pirate' 23

How To Win A Bet 25

How To Make Your Own Soap 26

How To Write Your Name In Hieroglyphs 28

How To Play Musical Clothes 29

How To Avoid Being Chomped By A Hippo 30

How To Play 'Hopscotch' 32

How To Be Friends With A Vampire 34

How To Make A Delicious Breakfast In Bed 37

How To Avoid Being Struck By Lightning 39

How To Play Crazy Golf 40

How To Make A Fortune Finder 43

How To Make A No-Bake Birthday Cake 47

How To Teach Your Cat To Sit 48

How To Survive On A Desert Island 50

How To Make Chocolate Brownies 53

How To Come Top In Spelling Tests 54

How To Dowse For Water 56

How To Set A World Record 57

How To Make A Paper Flower 59

How To Survive An Avalanche 60

How To Make Stalactites And Stalagmites 62

How To Fly A Paper Helicopter 63

How To Make A Piñata   66

How to Make Chocolate
Pecan Fudge   68

How To Tell If Someone Is
Telling The Truth   69

How To Write 'Happy
Birthday' In Ten
Different Languages   71

How To Read Someone's Mind 72

How To Host Your Own
Awards Ceremony   74

How To Play A Cool Card
Game   76

How To Make A Fizzy Drink   77

How To Survive A Shoal Of
Piranhas   78

How To Make A Step-Pyramid
Cake   80

How To Make A Pop-Up Card   83

How To Create Your Own
Lightning   85

How To Make A Fake Fossil   86

How To Make Your Own
Paper   88

How To Play 'Truth Or Dare'
. . . And Survive   90

How To Bling Up Your Bag   92

How To Make Up A Rope
Routine   94

How To Count In Roman
Numerals   96

How To Survive A Rip
Current   98

How To Measure A Tree   100

How To Build A Gingerbread
House   101

How To Skim Stones   104

How To Make A Photo
Frame   106

How To Make Friends With
A Yeti   108

How To Make An Origami
Box   110

How To Become A Famous
Actress   112

How To Know Your
Birth-Month Flower   114

How To Read Tea Leaves   115

How To Avoid A Shark
Attack   116

How To Dust For Fingerprints   118

How To Play 'What's In
The Bag?'   120

How To Build A House
Of Cards   121

How To Make Butterfly Cakes   123

How To Decorate Your Nails   125

HOW TO FLIP A PANCAKE

Demonstrate your amazing chef skills by making and flipping a pancake. Here's how ...

You Will Need:

- 125 g plain flour • 300 ml milk • an egg • olive oil
- a tasty topping • a fantastic flipping technique

WHAT YOU DO

1. Add the flour and milk to a mixing bowl.

2. Crack the egg and pour this into the bowl. Mix the ingredients together until the mixture (called 'batter') is smooth and has no lumps.

3. Pour about a teaspoonful of oil into a frying pan and heat. Ask for help from an adult with this bit, as the oil needs to get quite hot. Tilt the pan and move it in a circular motion so a thin layer of oil spreads out and covers the bottom of the pan. Turn down the heat to a medium setting.

4. Add two dessertspoonfuls of the batter mixture to the frying pan and tip the pan so that the mixture covers the base.

5. After about a minute's cooking time, check to see if the underside is cooked – lift the pan from the heat and give it a shake. If the pancake comes away from the bottom of the pan, it's time to flip.

6. Take the pan off the heat and tilt it away from you so that the pancake starts to slide (you might need to use both hands to hold the handle).

7. Now quickly pull the pan back towards you and upwards at the same time. Hopefully your pancake will flip up and over. Watch it as it does and be ready to move the pan up or down so that the pancake lands flat and not while it's twisting. If you're lucky, the pancake will flip 180°, ready to return to the heat and cook on the other side. If you're not lucky, it'll fall on the floor or stick to the ceiling.

Practice makes perfect. This mixture makes about a dozen or so pancakes, so you should manage to get it right by the time you're on to your second batch. When you do manage it, give yourself a huge round of applause.

SCOFFING

The best part of pancake-making is eating them. Here are some delicious toppings to add to your pancakes:

• Sweet toppings: a squeeze of lemon juice and a sprinkle of sugar; maple syrup and ice cream; chocolate sauce; puréed fruit (raspberries work especially well).

• Savoury toppings: sautéed mushrooms, leeks or tomatoes; baked beans; grated cheese.

HOW TO WORK OUT YOUR DOG'S 'HUMAN AGE'

A dog can be a girl's best friend, but your canine pal grows up a bit faster than you. Here are some ways of calculating the age of a dog in human terms.

A well-known method says that one dog year is equal to seven human years. Except that at one, a dog is more like a teenager, and almost fully grown – unlike a seven-year-old human.

A more accurate method, for breeds of dog that have an average lifespan of about 12 years, is to start with the age of 15 for the dog's first year, add ten years for its second, and then add five for each year of the dog's life after that.

AGE OF DOG	'HUMAN AGE'
1	15
2	25
3	30
4	35
5	40
6	45
7	50

Top Tip. For breeds of dog with a longer or shorter lifespan than 12 years, you'll need to adjust the formula slightly. Use a '15, 10, 3' formula for a longer-lived dog (such as toy poodles, or miniature dachshunds), or a '15, 10, 7' formula for a dog with a shorter lifespan (such as Irish Wolf Hounds and Great Danes).

HOW TO MAKE YOUR OWN CHRISTMAS CRACKERS

Everyone loves pulling crackers at Christmas and groaning at the corny jokes. They're easy to make, and the best bit is that you get to choose what goes inside. Here's how to make one ...

You Will Need:

- wrapping paper • scissors • two toilet roll tubes
- cracker snaps (available from most craft shops)
- glue or sticky tape • ribbon
- goodies to go inside the crackers (see page 12)

WHAT YOU DO

1. Cut out a rectangle of wrapping paper – its length should be equal to two and a half times the length of your toilet roll, and it should be wide enough to go around it one and a half times. Place the rectangle on a flat surface, patterned-side down.

2. Cut one of the toilet roll tubes in half. Place the two halves either side of the whole roll with a 5 cm gap between them along one of the long edges of the wrapping paper, as shown. Place the cracker snap on the paper beside them.

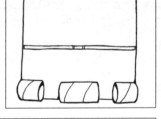

3. Roll the wrapping paper around the tubes and neatly glue or tape the join.

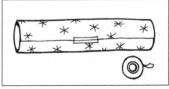

4. Carefully pinch the paper between one end of the tube and the half tube. Tie it with ribbon.

5. Put your goodies inside the open end of the cracker. Make sure your goodies aren't too heavy.

CRACKING CONTENTS

- a slip of paper with a terrible joke on it (see opposite)
- a paper crown
- small pens, pencils or erasers
- sample-size sachets of shampoo, bubble bath or moisturiser – the kind that come free in magazines
- hair bands or clips
- wrapped sweets (if you're including chocolates, remember not to leave the finished cracker anywhere warm)
- a balloon
- glitter or confetti (to make a sparkly shower when you pull the cracker)

6. Carefully pinch the paper between the other end of the tube and the half tube to secure the goodies inside your cracker (and to stop anyone from peeking). Tie it with more ribbon.

SOME TRULY AWFUL CRACKER JOKES

Here are some seasonal jokes to make you cringe. Pop them on a piece of paper and slip them into your crackers.

Which of Santa's reindeer can jump higher than a house?
They all can – houses can't jump.

What happens if you eat Christmas decorations?
You get tinsel-itus.

What's a monkey's favourite Christmas song?
Jungle Bells.

How does a snowman travel?
By icicle.

What's Santa's favourite pizza?
One that's deep pan, crisp and even.

On which side do turkeys have the most feathers?
On the outside.

HOW TO PLAY
THE NAME GAME

The 'Name Game' is a fun way to while away a rainy afternoon or lunch break – it will soon have you and your friends in fits of giggles.

HOW TO PLAY

1. Everyone must think of the name of a famous person, or a TV, film or book character, and write the name down on a sticky note.

2. Turn to the person on your right and stick your sticky note on their forehead (make sure they don't see the name written on it).

3. The youngest person in the room goes first. She has to guess the name on the sticky note on her forehead. She can only ask questions that have a 'yes' or 'no' answer. For example, 'Am I a man?' or 'Am I a soap star?' If the answer to any question is 'No', her turn is over and it's the next person's turn to guess their celebrity name.

4. The winner is the first to guess who they are. Keep playing until everyone finds out.

Top Tip. If you and your friends are having trouble guessing, narrow down the choices by deciding only to use movie stars, or only soap stars, or only TV characters.

HOW TO REMEMBER THE PLANETS IN THE SOLAR SYSTEM

There are nine planets in our solar system, right? Wrong! In 2006, Pluto was demoted from a planet to a 'dwarf planet', so there are now just eight.

Starting with the planet closest to the Sun, they are:

Mercury Venus Earth Mars Jupiter Saturn Uranus Neptune

To help you memorize the planets in the correct order, use one of these strange sentences:

My **V**ery **E**ducated **M**other **J**ust **S**erved **U**p **N**ewts

or

My **V**ole **E**ats **M**other's **J**am **S**andwiches **U**ncommonly **N**icely.

The first letter of each word matches the first letter of each planet. This method of remembering information is called a 'mnemonic'.

Why not make up your own mnemonics?

HOW TO MAKE SPAGHETTI JELLYFISH

Easy to make and seriously hilarious to serve, these spaghetti jellyfish will soon be your favourite supper treat.

You Will Need:
(For two people)
• two jumbo frankfurters • dried spaghetti

WHAT YOU DO

1. Cut each frankfurter into three equally sized pieces.

2. Break 24 strands of long spaghetti in half – so you have 48 shorter pieces of spaghetti. Push eight pieces of spaghetti into each piece of frankfurter – don't poke them all the way through.

3. Heat a saucepan of water until it is bubbling fiercely, then drop in your jellyfish and cook for seven minutes.

4. Remove each jellyfish with a slotted spoon and pop them on a plate. Enjoy them plain or with sauce.

HOW TO CONFUSE YOUR BRAIN AND BODY

There are many ways to confuse your brain and your body. Here are two simple methods to try out on a friend.

SAY WHEN

Ask your friend to hold her bare left arm out straight with the inside of her elbow facing upwards. Tell her that you are going to stroke your finger up the skin of her arm and she must shout when your finger reaches the dip at the inside of her elbow.

Ask her to close her eyes and concentrate. Start stroking the inside of her arm above her wrist. Gradually work your way up to the dip until she says stop. Chances are she'll find it hard to be accurate.

MIX UP

Ask your friend to stretch out her arms, and cross one over the other so her palms are pressed together.

Tell her to interlace her fingers, then bring her hands down and under, so she can hold them next to her chest.

Ask her to move the middle finger of her right hand. You can point to the finger, but don't touch it. She will probably find it hard to do, as her brain is confused by the strange position of her fingers.

HOW TO HIDE YOUR SECRET PAPERS

Every girl has at least one or two top-secret documents. Here's an easy way to keep them safe from prying eyes.

You Will Need:

- a large glass jar with a screw-on lid
- a toilet-roll tube • a pair of scissors
- buttons, beads or sweets

WHAT YOU DO

1. Place the toilet roll tube beside the jar and mark the height of the jar on the cardboard.

2. Cut across the roll width-ways about two centimetres below the mark you made.

3. Pop the roll in the glass jar. The top of it should be just below the top of the jar, so you can still screw the lid on.

4. Fill the space around the toilet roll with buttons, beads or sweets until the roll is hidden.

5. Slip your secret papers inside the toilet roll and replace the lid to keep your secrets safe.

HOW TO MAKE AMAZING MUESLI

You can make your own muesli – it's delicious and healthy and it couldn't be simpler to create. Try out the following recipe, then adjust the ingredients to your own taste.

You Will Need:

- 400 g porridge oats
- 50 g wheat bran
- 50 g oat bran
- 150 g of your favourite dried fruit – such as raisins, dried cranberries, dried apricots or sultanas
- 50 g toasted flaked almonds
- 25 g chopped walnuts
- 25 g sunflower seeds
- 25 g desiccated coconut

WHAT YOU DO

1. Put all the ingredients in a big bowl and mix them together.

2. Spoon out a bowlful for yourself and eat it with milk, or a mixture of milk and yoghurt.

3. Store your muesli in an airtight container and it should keep for a month or so.

Top Tip. For extra flavour, try a sprinkling of cinnamon on top of your muesli, or a spoonful of honey. You could add a chopped banana or another fresh fruit, too, when you serve it.

HOW TO PERFORM THE HEIMLICH MANOEUVRE

One day you might find yourself eating your lunch at school or in a restaurant, when someone begins to choke. You could save their life using a useful first-aid technique called the 'Heimlich Manoeuvre'.

ACT QUICKLY

A choking victim usually has a small object, such as a piece of food, lodged in their windpipe. They can't speak or breathe easily, so you need to act fast.

1. Ask them to lean forward and try to cough it out. If this doesn't work, approach the victim from behind and wrap your arms around their middle.

2. Form a fist with one hand and put the thumb side of the fist above the victim's navel and underneath their ribcage.

3. With the other hand, grab your fist and press it into the victim's stomach.

4. Use a sudden, quick, upward movement. Don't squeeze with your arms – just use pressure from your hands. This should force the object out of the windpipe. If it doesn't, keep going until it works.

Warning. This technique should be used only on an adult who is choking, and must only ever be used in an emergency. If not performed correctly the person you are supposed to be rescuing could be hurt.

HOW TO TELL WHICH WAY IS NORTH

Telling which way is north is a useful skill that will impress family or friends when you are out and about. Here's how:

HANDY IN BOTH HEMISPHERES

You'll need a watch (one with hands, not the digital kind) and you'll also need to be able to see where the sun is, which doesn't necessarily mean it has to be a sunny day. (NEVER look directly at the sun, not even on a cloudy day, because you could seriously damage your eyes.)

Hold the watch flat in the palm of your hand and rotate it until the hour hand is pointing in the direction of the sun.

In the northern hemisphere, the sun is due south at midday. You can work out the north–south line by dividing the angle between the hour hand (the little hand pointing to the position of the sun) and the number 12 on the watch face.

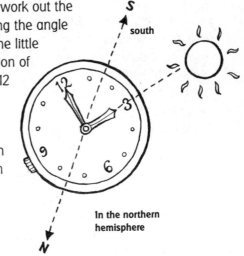

In the northern hemisphere

In this example, it's three o'clock, so the north-south line runs halfway between the 1 and 2 on the watch face. This tells you that in the northern hemisphere, due south is halfway between the 1 and the 2, so due north is halfway between the 7 and the 8.

In the southern hemisphere, the sun is due north at midday, so in the example on page 21, due north will be between the 1 and the 2.

A STRING THING

If you don't have a watch at all, find north by putting a stick in the ground and measuring its shadow at different times of day.

You Will Need:

- a long, straight stick • two medium-sized pebbles
- some level ground • a piece of string • a twig

1. Place the stick in the ground and mark the tip of the stick's shadow in the morning with one pebble.

2. Draw a semi-circular line around the stick (to do this, tie a piece of string to the stick and a twig to the other end and mark the ground). The line should be the same distance away from the stick as the pebble.

3. The stick's shadow will get shorter as the time gets closer to 12 noon, and longer as the afternoon goes on. Wait until the stick's shadow touches the edge of the semi-circle again and mark the point with your second pebble.

4. As the sun moves across the sky from east to west the shadow from the stick will move in the opposite direction, from west to east. The line between your morning pebble and your evening pebble marks a line from west to east, so if you draw another line at a right angle to this, you will also have north and south.

HOW TO SPEAK 'PIRATE'

Avast thar, landlubbers. So, ye be wantin' to speak like a pirate? Yarr! First, you'll be learnin' some pirate vocabulary, then you'll be discoverin' yer own true pirate name.

PIRATE VOCABULARY

Ahoy ... Hello

Avast ... Stop

Bilge rat ... Rat that lives in the lowest, slimiest part of the ship – used as an insult

Booty ... Treasure

Cat o' nine tails ... Whip used in seafaring punishment

Davy Jones's locker ... The bottom of the ocean

Doubloons ... Gold pieces

Fiddler's Green ... Pirate heaven

Galley ... Kitchen

Grog ... Alcoholic drink

Hearty ... Friend (as in 'me hearty')

Hornswaggler ... Cheat
Jolly Roger ... Pirate flag
Keelhauling ... Dragging someone along the bottom
of the ship as a punishment
Landlubber ... Someone not
used to life at sea ('land lover')
Matey ... Friend/shipmate
Pieces of eight ... Silver coins
cut into eight pieces
**Scurvy dog/Scurvy
cur** ... Sick dog, used
as an insult
Shiver me timbers! ...
Exclamation of surprise
Walkin' the plank ...
Making someone walk on
to a plank and off the side
of the ship, preferably into
shark-infested waters, as
punishment
Yarr! ... General
exclamation, usually
positive.

YOUR PIRATE NAME

Add a tenth name to each of the columns opposite. Choose
three numbers between 1 and 10, then look up the three
names that correspond to those numbers – choose one from
each of the three columns opposite. Put the three names
together and you'll have your pirate name. Get your friends to
do it, too.

1	Captain	Bess	Blackheart
2	Crazy	Kate	Flint
3	First Mate	Peg	Morgan
4	Bloodthirsty	Mary	Cutlass
5	Ruthless	Mags	Kidd
6	Stinky	Ann	Bonny
7	Peg-leg	Flora	Finnegan
8	Fearless	Nell	Silver
9	Daring	Pearl	Braveheart
10	....	....	....

HOW TO WIN A BET

Here are a couple of bets you can be almost sure you will win.

DOUGHNUT CHALLENGE

This is a delicious dare – buy some sugar doughnuts. Bet your friends that they cannot eat one without licking their lips. It is almost impossible, so you should be able to win back the money the doughnuts cost you.

YOU'D HAVE TO BE CRACKERS

Challenge your friends that they cannot eat three cream crackers (these are really dry biscuits that are usually eaten with cheese) in one minute without taking a sip of water. Very few people manage to do this, but one man has managed it in just under 15 seconds – so one of your friends may surprise you.

HOW TO MAKE YOUR OWN SOAP

Decorative soaps are a lovely gift and they're easy to make yourself, which makes them even more special. Here is a simple method to make your own soaps in colours, scents and shapes you've designed yourself.

You Will Need:

• a natural glycerine soap bar • a cheese grater
• a jug you can put in the microwave
• food colouring in the colour of your choice • a spoon
• essential oils of your choice • soap moulds (you can buy these from a craft shop or use an ice-cube tray – these come in a variety of shapes and will make funky soap cubes)

WHAT YOU DO

1. Use the grater to shred the soap into small pieces (get help from an adult with this as you don't want grated fingers). Put the pieces into a jug. Ask an adult to place the jug in the microwave and heat it on full power for about one minute.

2. Using an oven glove, remove the jug from the microwave. Stir a few drops of food colouring into the melted soap, until it looks a pretty colour.

3. Add a few drops of essential oil. Try lavender and tea tree, geranium and orange, orange and lemon, or lavender, geranium and bergamot.

4. Give your soap mixture another stir, then pour it into your moulds. It will set in about an hour and you can remove it from the mould.

Top Tips. Try making multi-coloured soaps. Pour a little of one colour into your mould, leave it to dry before adding a different coloured layer, then another colour on top of that. Alternatively you could add some glitter into your soap mixture before it sets.

HOW TO WRITE YOUR NAME IN HIEROGLYPHS

Hieroglyphic script was used thousands of years ago by the Ancient Egyptians. Some hieroglyphs represented whole words, while others represented sounds or groups of sounds. It took Egyptian scribes years to learn how to write using hieroglyphs. You don't have that long, so here's a simplified version of Egyptian hieroglyphs in which there is a symbol for each letter of the alphabet.

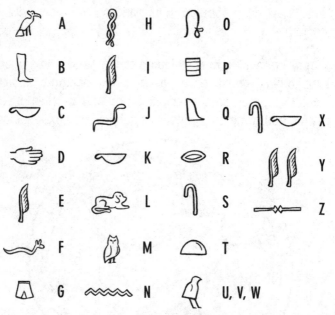

Use the symbols to spell out your name in the box below.

HOW TO PLAY MUSICAL CLOTHES

'Musical Clothes' is very similar to 'Musical Chairs', except when the game is over you end up looking very silly indeed.

All you need is a bag full of old clothes in as many different sizes and types as you can find. The more crimes against fashion the better. Coats, hats, earmuffs, jumpers, T-shirts, bras, trousers, skirts, shorts and shoes – get your friends to bring a few items each.

You need one volunteer to control the music, while everyone else sits in a circle.

When the music starts, pass the bag of clothes around the circle. When the music stops, the person holding the bag has to shut her eyes, rummage in the bag, pull out an item of clothing and put it on.

The music starts again, and the game continues until all the clothes in the bag have been used up.

At this point, the friend controlling the music gets to choose the winner – the person who looks silliest!

HOW TO AVOID BEING CHOMPED BY A HIPPO

If you think hippos are fun-loving, chilled-out mud-wallowers, think again – they can be very aggressive. They tend to attack if they think someone is trespassing on their territory. They are huge animals, weighing as much as four tonnes, with razor-sharp tusk-like teeth. Hippos have even been known to bite crocodiles in half.

Bearing all this in mind, you might want to stay away from hippo habitats, but here are a few tips just in case:

EMERGENCY TACTICS

• Keep as far away from the hippo as you can. There are two types of hippo to avoid particularly – female hippos protecting their young and hungry hippos short of food during a drought.

• If a hippo opens its vast jaws, it's probably not yawning – far from being bored, the animal is showing you that it has

very big teeth and could attack at any moment. Make sure you heed this aggressive warning.

• Show that you're not a threat by backing away slowly. If the hippo sees that you're moving out of its territory by yourself, it might not feel the need to help you on your way by taking a large bite out of you.

• Try and make sure you're downwind of the hippo, so that the wind isn't carrying your scent straight up the hippo's nostrils, and sending angry messages to its brain.

• Never block a hippo's path to water. This is guaranteed to make it cross, which should definitely be avoided.

• Running away won't do you much good, because a hippo will easily outrun you. As a last resort, run as fast as you can to the nearest tree – climb it and shout for help.

HOW TO PLAY 'HOPSCOTCH'

Girls have been playing 'Hopscotch' for centuries (not the same girls, obviously). It's a fun and easy game for two to four players, plus all the hopping involved will help you keep fit.

The most common layout created to play 'Hopscotch' uses squares – alternately one square then two, finishing with a semicircle at the top to make a total of ten, as shown below. You can play hopscotch anywhere that you can chalk out this layout. Alternatively, if you have paving stones near your house, adapt the pattern to fit them.

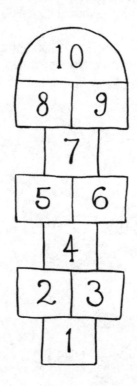

You Will Need:

• chalk • a pebble or stone
• a hard outside surface to play on

HOW TO PLAY

1. Draw the layout of the 'Hopscotch' pattern, either by chalking it onto the ground, or marking it out in the dirt with a stick.

2. Number the squares 1 to 9, and 10 at the top.

3. To start, throw the pebble on to square 1. Make sure the pebble lands cleanly inside the box – if it lands touching a line your turn is already over.

4. Jump over the square containing your pebble, landing with your left foot in the 2 square and your right in 3. Continue, alternately hopping and jumping until you reach the semicircle marked 10. Then turn (balancing on one foot) to make your way back to your pebble. Stop on squares 2 and 3 to pick the pebble up before jumping over square 1 to complete the course.

5. If you touch a line with your foot, lose your balance, or miss a square, your turn is over. When it comes back to your turn you have to start from square 1 again.

6. Each time you successfully finish the course, throw your pebble to the next square in sequence. So your next throw would be into square 2. Hop on one foot through squares 1, 3 and 4.

Top Tip. Find an odd-shaped stone, with a flat side which will not roll, and practise accurate throwing skills.

HOW TO BE FRIENDS WITH A VAMPIRE

You may have read a vampire book, or seen a film or TV show about them, but how easy would it really be to have a vampire for a friend? If you don't mind their eating habits, try these helpful pointers to be a vampire's perfect pal.

BLENDING IN

To make your vampire friend feel at ease and to help them blend in, wear dark clothes yourself. Blood red is a great colour for accessories, and a floor-length cape is a fashion-must. Why not knit your friend some gloves, a hat and a scarf? Vampires are dead and therefore have no blood circulation, so their skin is constantly cold to the touch.

OUT AND ABOUT

Don't suggest meeting up at midday. All your meetings with your new 'BF' will have to take place under cover of darkness, as they can't stand the sun.

Never take your vampire friend to the hairdresser's, or anywhere else where there are a lot of mirrors – a vampire's lack of a reflection is guaranteed to cause widespread panic. The whole lack-of-reflection thing may also mean that your friend looks a little ungroomed. Find tactful ways of pointing out any appearance blunders, such as bad-hair days or cabbage between their front teeth.

Eating out can be a problem – avoid ordering garlic bread. Vampires hate garlic and will run screaming from it, causing an embarrassing scene. As your friend only really fancies blood, they might find it hard to pick something on the menu. Blood pudding – a traditional dish – or raw steak is probably their

favourite food (when ordering, don't confuse steak and stake – the wooden instrument used to kill vampires by plunging it through their hearts).

If you cut your finger while carving your meal, beware. The smell of blood will drive your friend crazy and could put them off their pudding.

PARTY TIME

If you invite your vampire friend to your birthday party, there are certain things to remember. Don't ask them to help you blow up the balloons before your party – they are dead and have no breath.

Make sure you answer the door when they arrive – vampires can only come in to your house if they are invited. If someone else answers the doorbell, there could be confusion and delay.

Don't ask your vampire pal to pose with your possie for photos – their image cannot be captured on film.

If you are throwing a party specially for your undead friend, avoid baking a birthday cake and adding candles. Vampires survive for hundreds of years and your pal might feel self-conscious if you try to fit 207 candles on the cake.

HOW TO MAKE A DELICIOUS BREAKFAST IN BED

If you want to give your mum or dad a really special treat – perhaps for Mothers' Day or Fathers' Day – breakfast in bed is guaranteed to please.

You Will Need:

- a tray • a pretty tea towel
- crockery and cutlery • a napkin
- muesli • milk • different kinds of fruit
- plain yogurt • a glass • fruit juice
- toast • butter • jam or honey • tea or coffee
- a single flower

WHAT YOU DO

1. Make your breakfast tray look as good as possible by lining it with a pretty tea towel (this will also make the items on the tray less likely to slip). Use the nicest crockery, cutlery, napkin and glass that you're allowed to get your hands on.

2. Add a bowl of muesli with a small jug of milk next to it. You could try making your own muesli for this (see page 19). If your mum or dad isn't keen on muesli, make them a fruit salad instead. Chop any of the following fruits you can find in to a bowl – a banana, an apple, a tangerine and some raspberries, strawberries or blueberries. Add a dollop of plain yogurt on top.

3. Fill a glass with fruit juice and add that to the tray, too.

4. Toast a slice or two of bread, and cut them in half diagonally. Put the toast triangles on a plate, together with a small pat of butter and a jar of jam or honey.

5. Don't forget a cup of breakfast tea, herbal tea, or coffee (make sure there is enough milk in the jug for your parent to add some to their hot drink).

6. Add a flower as a fabulous finishing touch.

Top Tip. Your mum or dad might also love a newspaper or a favourite magazine to go with their breakfast.

HOW TO AVOID BEING STRUCK BY LIGHTNING

Lightning is an electrical charge travelling between a thundercloud and the Earth, which you see as bright flashes in the sky during storms. The chances of actually being struck by lightning are millions to one, but that doesn't mean you shouldn't take care in certain situations. Here's how to avoid getting a serious singeing …

- Lightning will always find the quickest way to the ground. A tall tree, or even your body, are all quicker ways for the lightning to reach the ground than travelling through the air. So the best advice is to stay indoors during a thunderstorm.

- If you're inside a vehicle, stay there. The lightning will be more attracted to the metal vehicle than it will be to you. Make sure you have the doors closed and the windows up, and don't touch anything metal inside the vehicle.

- If you do find yourself outside, stay away from water, high, exposed ground, and tall objects such as flag poles. Don't carry anything that makes you taller, especially if it's made of metal – so golf clubs and umbrellas are best avoided. If you time the delay between seeing a flash of lightning and hearing the roll of thunder that follows, you can tell how far away the storm is. Every three seconds you count is equivalent to one kilometre and every five seconds is one mile. If the delay is less than 15 seconds, the storm is nearby, so take evasive action quickly. If there's no shelter within easy reach, crouch down low and stay where you are until the storm passes.

HOW TO PLAY CRAZY GOLF

Set up a mini crazy-golf course inside your house for a rainy-day sport that won't involve you and your friends getting wet at all.

You'll need a fair bit of space, so make sure you're not going to be using rooms needed by other members of your family.

You Will Need:

• a golf club (an umbrella, a broom or a walking stick will work fine if you don't have the real thing) • a sheet of paper • a saucepan • anything that can act as a 'hazard ' - such as boxes, cardboard tubes, CD cases, books, silver baking foil, etc • masking tape • sticky tape • a small rubber ball (don't use a golf ball - they are too hard to use indoors)

WHAT YOU DO

1. Work out a 'hole' – this is the route each player must follow. The route can start in one room and end in another. It should involve going round, under and over tables, chairs and sofas, and even down stairs. It can stretch through doorways – which the ball must pass through without touching the door or frame. It can include bouncing the ball off spots on the skirting board marked with masking tape.

2. Mark the beginning of your route with a circle cut from paper, and mark the end of your route with a saucepan – the ball must be putted into this to finish.

3. Remove anything breakable from the areas of the house you're using.

4. Put in some 'hazards'. These could include:

- Cardboard tubes to knock the ball through
- Boxes that players have to bounce the ball off in a particular order
- Books or CD cases that the player must zigzag the ball between
- A long sheet of baking foil crinkled up, then laid out flat on the floor and stuck down with sticky tape – this makes it difficult to control the route of the ball.
- Boxes with 'gates' cut into the sides that players have to knock the ball through.

Top Tip. Creating a good course will involve some trial and error. When you think you've finished, give the course a trial run without scoring and see if anything needs to change – perhaps some elements of the course are just too difficult, while others are too easy.

HOW TO PLAY

Each player putts (gently hits) the ball around the course with the golf club, negotiating all the obstacles and hazards. A record is kept of how many times each player has to hit the ball before it finally ends up in the saucepan.

A penalty point is added if a player has to pick up the ball and move it because it's become trapped somewhere.

When everyone has completed the whole course, the number of hits and penalty points are added together for each player, and the player with the lowest number wins!

HOW TO MAKE A FORTUNE FINDER

If your friends are wondering what might happen to them in the future, find out for them, using this fun fortune finder and your amazing skills of prediction!

You Will Need:

• a square piece of paper • a pen

WHAT YOU DO

1. Fold the paper in half diagonally.

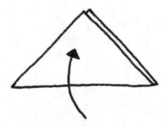

2. Do the same again to make a smaller triangle, then unfold, and lay it flat.

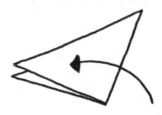

3. Fold each corner of the square into the centre, so the corners all meet at the middle.

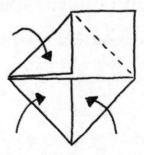

4. Turn the paper over and do the same again, folding each corner into the centre so that they meet in the middle.

5. Turn the paper over so that you can see four squares. Fold the paper in half down the middle, with the squares on the outside.

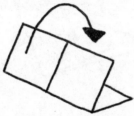

6. Open the paper out so you can see the four squares again. Now fold the paper down the middle the other way.

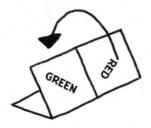

7. Write the name of four different colours on the four squares, then turn the fortune finder over. Write a different number on each of the eight triangles.

8. Lift up the triangles and write down a fortune for each number – how about 'You will become a billionaire'; 'You will live in Australia'; 'You will have six children'; 'You will fall in love when you are 19'; or 'You will become a famous surgeon'?

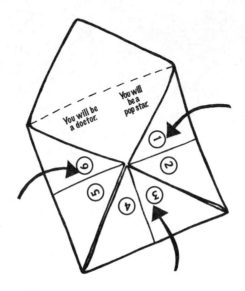

USING YOUR FORTUNE FINDER

Now you have your fortune finder – it's time to tell a friend's fortune. Slide your thumbs and forefingers under the four outside flaps and push the points of your fortune finder into the centre, so you can see the four colours.

Ask a friend to choose a colour. Spell out the name of the colour, while opening and closing the fortune finder for each letter.

When you come to the last letter, hold the fortune finder open and ask your friend to choose one of the numbers revealed. Count out that number, opening and closing the fortune finder as before.

Ask your friend to pick another number, and open the flap with that number on it. Then simply read your friend's fortune.

HOW TO MAKE A NO-BAKE BIRTHDAY CAKE

If it's your friend's birthday and you really want to spoil her, why not have a go at making a birthday cake? This one is delicious – and you don't even have to bake it.

You Will Need:

- 175 g digestive biscuits
- 75 g butter • 225 g cream cheese
- 150 ml strawberry yogurt • 150 ml double cream
- a dozen ripe strawberries

WHAT YOU DO

1. First the really fun part – put your biscuits into a plastic food bag and bash them with a rolling pin to make crumbs.

2. Melt the butter in a saucepan and stir in the biscuit crumbs you have created. Ask an adult to help, as you want to avoid any burnt fingers.

3. Tip the mixture into the bottom of a 20 cm flan dish and press it down with the back of a spoon to make a flat base.

4. When it's cool, put it in the fridge for half an hour or so, until it has hardened.

5. In a large bowl, mix together the cream cheese and yogurt.

6. Whisk the double cream in a separate bowl, until it makes stiff peaks (you may find this easier with an electric whisk).

7. Now gently 'fold' the whisked cream into the cheese and yogurt, stirring once around the bowl and once through the middle with the side of a wooden spoon. Continue this action until all the cream is mixed in.

8. Tip the cream cheese, yogurt and cream mixture on top of the biscuit base. Spread it out evenly, then put it back in the fridge until the filling is firm – about 30 minutes.

9. Slice the strawberries and arrange them in a pattern on top of the cake.

10. Add some birthday candles.

Top Tip. You could use different fruit to suit the taste of the birthday girl – raspberries or blueberries are both good choices.

HOW TO TEACH YOUR CAT TO SIT

Many people think our feline friends are impossible to train because of their independent air, but it's not true – you really can teach your cat to sit.

WHAT YOU DO

1. Before you start, make sure your cat is feeling relaxed and happy. Stroke it to make it feel comfortable.

2. Show your cat an edible treat (such as a cat biscuit) and say, 'Fluffy [use your cat's name], sit!'

3. Move the treat back over the cat's head. As it watches the treat it should sit down to balance – if it doesn't, gently press down on its hind quarters.

4. As it sits, give lots of praise, and the treat.

Given time, your cat will learn that when it sits it gets the treat, and it'll do it without you moving it over its head. Be patient and keep practising. If you find that either you or the cat is becoming frustrated, leave it 'til another time.

Top Tip. You may get better results if you train your cat shortly before feeding time.

HOW TO SURVIVE ON A DESERT ISLAND

Have you ever thought about what you'd do if you were marooned on a desert island? Here's how to make the best of the situation until help arrives ...

THIRSTY WORK

Nobody can survive for more than a few days without drinking water. In the heat of a desert island, you will be sweating a lot and dehydrating rapidly. Finding water is your first priority.

With luck there will be fresh water flowing on your island. Search along the shore for a stream running into the sea. Follow the stream back towards its source as far as you can. When you can go no further, check that the water is running clear and that it doesn't smell bad before you drink any. Only drink a tiny amount at first and increase day by day. This allows you to check it is safe to drink before you have consumed too much.

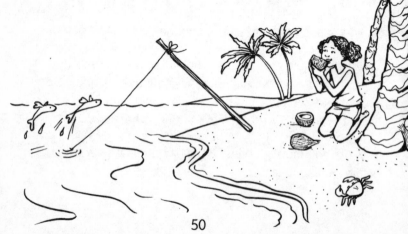

If you can't find a source of fresh water, you will need to collect water. There are two main methods. First, make sure you have any containers available positioned to collect rainwater when it falls. Store the water somewhere cold and shady during the day to stop it evaporating. Second, every morning you should collect the dew that has formed on the leaves of plants – this is perfect for drinking. Mop it up with a clean cloth and wring the cloth into a container.

TAKE SHELTER

It is essential to stay out of the heat of the sun on your island, so the next thing to do is make a shelter. Look for something that could form the basis of your shelter, such as a dry rocky outcrop, a fallen tree, or even a cave. Gather reeds, twigs, and large leaves and use them to finish your shelter. You could try weaving branches together. Line the shelter with dry leaves, pine needles or bracken.

FOOD

Some doctors say a human being can survive without food for four to six weeks. However, if you leave it for more than a few days you will be too weak to look for food when you need it. Why not make a fishing rod with string, a stick and a safety pin as a hook, and see if you have any luck landing a fish? Alternatively you could

attempt to spear fish with a sharpened stick. Failing that, most seaweed is edible, though you might have to boil it for a while.

Coconuts are a great source of food and drink, and hopefully

these will be falling from the trees on your island. The skill is to open them.

1. Once you have removed the green outer layer, pull off the 'husk' – the hairy outer layer.

2. At one end of the coconut, you'll see three dents – like two eyes and a mouth. Hold that end in one hand. Find the 'seam' that runs between the eyes. Follow the seam to the middle of the coconut. Imagine a line running around its fattest part.

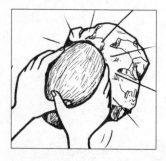

3. Find a large rock and give the coconut some hard taps along this line. Keep turning the coconut so you hit it all the way round the seam. After a few good whacks, the coconut should break into two halves.

4. Scrape out the white 'meat' inside with a sharp shell or piece of rock. Smell the inside of the coconut before you eat it. If it smells sour or mouldy, throw it away.

HOW TO MAKE CHOCOLATE BROWNIES

These brownies make perfect sleepover treats – crisp on the outside, gooey on the inside, and chocolatey through and through.

You Will Need:
(To make 16 brownies)

- 100 g plain chocolate • 100 g unsalted butter (at room temperature) • 200 g caster sugar • two large eggs, beaten • 50 g plain flour • 25 g cocoa powder • a teaspoon of salt • a teaspoon of baking powder • 100 g chopped walnuts

WHAT YOU DO

1. Preheat the oven to 180°C/Gas Mark 4.

2. Break the chocolate into squares, then chop the squares into smaller pieces. Put all the chocolate in a saucepan with the butter and carefully melt it over a very low heat, stirring it slowly (you should get an adult to help you with melting things and when using the oven later).

3. Take the saucepan off the heat when the chocolate is melted, and add the sugar. Mix well.

4. Break the eggs into a small bowl and, with a fork or a whisk, stir them vigorously – this is called 'beating' the eggs. Then add the beaten eggs to the chocolate mixture and stir.

5. Mix the flour, cocoa powder, salt and baking powder

together in a bowl and then add them to the chocolate mixture.

6. Add the chopped walnuts and stir everything together until the mixture is smooth.

7. Pour the mixture into a 20 cm baking tin that has been lined with greased baking parchment. Smooth it out to the edges.

8. Wearing oven gloves, pop the baking tin in the oven and cook for 25 minutes, or until the top of the brownie mix is firm to the touch. All ovens are slightly different, so keep an eye on your brownies to make sure they don't burn.

9. Leave them to cool and then cut them into 16 squares to share with your family and friends.

HOW TO COME TOP IN SPELLING TESTS

The English language is difficult to spell because it doesn't follow a simple set of rules (well, not always). The 'spellchecker' you might have on your computer won't be any use to you in an exam or spelling test. There are no magic shortcuts to becoming a good speller, but here are some top tips.

• Read as much as you can – books, newspapers, comics, anything you can get your hands on. Take notice of the 'shape' of words on the page, so you will recognize if they are written incorrectly. If you come across a word that you've never seen written down before, try to memorize it. Follow the 'Look, Think, Cover, Write, Check' procedure: look at the word and think about it, then cover it up and see if you can write it out from memory – then check what you've written.

• Word games are great for improving your spelling. Play games such as Hangman, and tackle crosswords and word searches.

• Learn spelling rules, such as 'i before e except after c', but remember the exceptions, too. (There are always exceptions to every rule – with this rule they include neighbour, height and weird.)

• If you keep getting particular words wrong, why not make up a mnemonic (memory aid) to help you spell it? For example, remember 'There's A RAT in sepARATe'.

A QUICK TEST

If you want to give someone a hard spelling test, try these:

1. Consensus **2.** Embarrass **3.** Focused **4.** Foreign
5. Inoculate **6.** Liaison **7.** Liquefy **8.** Phlegm
9. Supersede **10.** Unnecessary

55

HOW TO DOWSE FOR WATER

Some people claim to be able to detect underground water, and other substances, such as oil or metal, by 'dowsing' for them. Dowsing means locating something that is hidden. Dowsing rods are used, which cross each other when they come near water. The two L-shaped pieces of metal shown below are made of two bits of wire from a coat hanger, with two lengths of straw threaded on to them to act as handles.

There's no evidence to prove that people really can find water by dowsing, but why not conduct your own experiment with friends?

You Will Need:

• dowsing rods • 10 plastic bottles
• 10 buckets or cardboard boxes • some water
• paper and a pen

WHAT YOU DO

1. Without any of your friends seeing, fill half the bottles with water and leave the rest empty.

2. Place the bottles about half a metre apart in a row. Cover each with a bucket or box. Number the buckets or boxes clearly.

3. Now ask one of your friends to walk along the row of buckets and tell you if her dowsing rods detect water under any of them. Make a note of which buckets she thinks are covering water and which she thinks are not.

4. When all your friends have done their dowsing, reveal the results.

HOW TO SET A WORLD RECORD

If you think you're the fastest, the slowest, the best, or maybe even the worst in the world, here's how to register a world record officially.

First you need to decide whether you want to set a new record or break an existing one? If you choose a completely new record, you will need to contact 'Guinness World Records', the organization that judges, records and publishes a famous book containing many world records every year. You can go to their website for all the details of registering a record-breaking attempt. You will find it at www.guinnessworldrecords.com.

Tell Guinness exactly what record attempt you are planning. They'll let you know if they think it's a suitable idea. If they do, they will detail exactly what evidence you need to provide to show you set the record fairly and squarely. If they think your idea is too dangerous or too difficult to prove, they won't accept it.

You may choose to break an existing record – and there are all sorts from which to choose – rolling an orange with your nose, egg-throwing and marathon kissing are all possibilities. Guinness will tell you the details of the current record, the guidelines you need to follow, and the evidence you need to provide. In some cases, they will send a someone to witness your record attempt.

Once you've submitted details of your record attempt, Guinness will let you know within a few weeks whether or not you've proved your claim. If you have, you are a record breaker!

HOW TO MAKE A PAPER FLOWER

These paper flowers are simple to make, and look great added as decoration to wrapped gifts.

You Will Need:

- four sheets of coloured tissue paper about 15 cm by 8 cm
- scissors • a length of thread

WHAT YOU DO

1. Lay the four sheets of tissue paper on top of one another. Fold them into a 'concertina' (by folding about 1 cm up then turning the tissue paper over and folding 1 cm back, and so on).

2. Use scissors to round off the straight edge at each end of your folded paper strip.

3. Squeeze the middle of the strip between your fingers, and tie it securely with cotton. Fan out each side.

4. Very carefully separate the four layers of tissue paper, and fluff them up to make a flower head.

HOW TO SURVIVE AN AVALANCHE

Snow avalanches occur when the snow on a mountain slope becomes so heavy that all it wants to do is travel downhill. Every year people perish under tonnes of sliding snow. So if you go skiing or snowboarding, you need to know how to avoid being caught out – especially since most avalanches are caused by the weight of a single person on unstable snow. Here are some tips:

BE PREPARED

Be alert. Before you hit the slopes, listen to the radio or TV for avalanche warnings in the area you are in.

On the slopes, look out for recent heavy snowfall and strong winds, rapid changes in temperature, cracks in the snow, and snow that sounds hollow. Avalanches are more likely to happen on steep, north-facing slopes. You might want to avoid them altogether.

Always carry a mobile phone to call for help, and an avalanche beacon – this is a piece of equipment that will tell rescuers where you are.

EMERGENCY TACTICS

Once you spot an avalanche speeding towards you, you need to act fast. Don't try to outrun the snow – the snow can travel at great speeds.

Drop all your ski poles as they may injure you when you fall. As the snow surrounds you, try to stay near the top of it by 'swimming' upwards towards the surface. Try to grab a tree or bush if you slide past them.

As the avalanche slows down, curl your body into a ball with your hands over your face. When you stop moving, quickly move your hands back and forwards to make an air space in front of your face with your hands. The snow sets hard within seconds, so this is very important.

Turn on your avalanche beacon and sit tight – help is on the way.

HOW TO MAKE STALACTITES AND STALAGMITES

Stalactites and stalagmites look a little like stone icicles. They hang from cave ceilings or rise from cave floors, and are formed by water dripping through limestone. With some basic supplies and a little patience, you can make one in your own kitchen.

You Will Need:

- two glass jars or plastic cups • some newspaper
- hot water • Epsom salts or bicarbonate of soda
- a spoon • three plastic plates • two paperclips
- 75 cm length of wool (or cotton string)

WHAT YOU DO

1. Find somewhere you can leave your experiment for at least a week without someone tidying it up. It can be messy, so don't use a surface that's easily damaged, and put down several layers of newspaper before you start.

2. Carefully fill one jar about three-quarters full with hot water. Add a few spoonfuls of Epsom salts or bicarbonate of soda, and stir until they are dissolved. Keep adding more salt or soda until no more will dissolve. Now do the same with the second jar.

3. Stand each jar on a plate on the newspaper, about 20 cm apart. Place another plate in between them.

4. Dip the wool or string into one of the jars. Fold the wool in half lengthways and twist it. Attach a paperclip to each end of the twisted wool.

5. Put either end of the wool into each of the jars, as shown below. Let it sag in the middle so that it dangles a few centimetres above the middle plate.

6. Leave your experiment alone for a few days, until your homemade stalactites and stalagmites form on the middle plate.

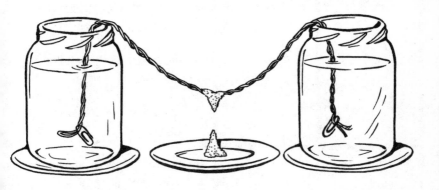

Top Tip. You could add food colouring to your salt or soda solutions and create coloured stalactites and stalagmites.

HOW TO FLY A PAPER HELICOPTER

This paper helicopter couldn't be simpler to make, and it's so much more interesting than a paper plane.

You Will Need:

• a sheet of paper • a pen • a ruler
• scissors • a paperclip

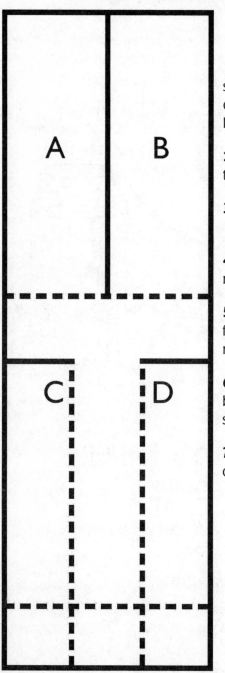

WHAT YOU DO

1. Trace this design on to the sheet of paper. The solid lines are cut lines and the dotted lines are fold lines.

2. Cut the shape out along the cut lines.

3. Fold along the dotted line 16 mm from the bottom.

4. Fold along the dotted line marked C.

5. Turn the paper over, fold along the dotted line marked D.

6. Slide a paperclip on to the base of your helicopter as shown.

7. Fold flap A towards you and flap B away from you.

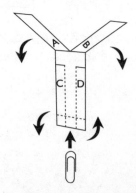

THROW

Your helicopter is ready to fly. Throw it into the air, paperclip end first, and watch it twirl through the air.

Get your friends to make helicopters and see who can keep theirs in the air longest.

Alternatively, draw a target on a sheet of paper. To do this, place a dinner plate on a sheet of paper and draw around it. Place a smaller plate in the middle of the circle and draw around that. Mark the inner circle as scoring 50 points and the outer scoring 25. Place your target on the floor and see how close you and your friends can land their helicopters to the inner circle.

HOW TO MAKE A PIÑATA

Make your next party a Mexican-style fiesta, and no fiesta would be complete without a piñata. A piñata is a decoration filled with sweets or small gifts. The best part is that a piñata has to be bashed open with a stick to get at the goodies.

You Will Need:

• a balloon • a piece of thick string at least 60 cm long
• newspaper • paintbrush • a mixture of 250 ml water and
250 ml PVA glue • a pin • scissors • sticky tape
• five sheets of A4 card • paperclips • poster paint
• a blindfold • a stick • tissue paper

WHAT YOU DO

1. Blow up your balloon and tie a knot in the neck. Rest the balloon in a small bowl to stop it wobbling about.

2. Tear the newspaper into strips, dip them in the PVA glue and water mixture and use them to cover the balloon completely. Wait until it's completely dry, then add another layer. Repeat until you have added five layers of newspaper.

3. Once the final layer is dry, cover the whole thing with the diluted glue and leave it overnight to dry thoroughly.

4. Pop the balloon inside using a pin. Cut a flap in the paper shell and remove the balloon. Check the inside of your piñata is dry, then fill it with sweets. Reseal the flap with sticky tape.

5. Use a sheet of card to make a cone shape and stick it with glue (secure it with paperclips while the glue dries). Cut off the triangular ends at the base of your cone. Repeat with the other four sheets of card.

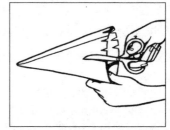

6. Take each cone and make small cuts, about 1 cm deep, around the base. Put glue on the underside of the flaps and use them to stick the cones to the piñata, making a star shape. You'll need to hold them in place to make sure they stick properly.

7. Once your star piñata is dry, paint it with brightly coloured poster paints.

Top Tip. For a truly Mexican look, decorate your piñata with strips of tissue paper with cuts 1 cm deep in them, to make a frill. Glue the uncut edges to the piñata, overlapping the strips each time.

SMASHING

Use the end of your scissors to pierce a hole in the top of your piñata. Attach the length of string and hang it from a tree branch or

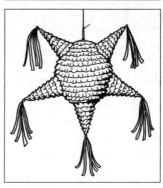

a washing line. Everyone takes a turn to be blindfolded and bash the piñata with a stick until it breaks.

HOW TO MAKE CHOCOLATE PECAN FUDGE

Create these simply delicious, chocolaty treats.

You Will Need:

- 450 g dark chocolate • 75 g unsalted butter (at room temperature) • 400 g tin sweetened condensed milk
- ½ teaspoon vanilla essence • 100 g of chopped pecan nuts

WHAT YOU DO

1. Chop the chocolate into squares. Then heat the chocolate, butter and condensed milk together in a saucepan over a low heat until the chocolate melts. Keep stirring and be careful not to let it burn. Get an adult to help so you don't singe your fingers.

2. Take the saucepan off the heat when the chocolate has melted and stir in the vanilla essence.

3. Stir in the chopped pecan nuts.

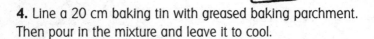

4. Line a 20 cm baking tin with greased baking parchment. Then pour in the mixture and leave it to cool.

5. Put the mixture in the fridge and leave it for an hour, or until it has completely set.

6. Cut the fudge into bite-sized pieces, and wrap each piece in baking parchment until you're ready to eat it.

HOW TO TELL IF SOMEONE IS TELLING THE TRUTH

It's impossible to know for sure whether a friend is being honest or telling a great big fib, but there are some classic tell-tale signs you can look out for to help you decide:

• A guilty person will often speak more than they do normally, adding lots of unnecessary details in an attempt to convince you of what they are saying. Look out for this or for your friend talking to avoid uncomfortable silences or pauses in the conversation.

• Is she touching her face, or tugging at her ear or hair a lot? Fidgeting, blinking and scratching are all signs of an unusual level of nervousness that might be caused by fibbing.

• Is your friend covering her mouth, nose or throat with her hand? This is a classic clue that she wants to hide her fibs.

• When people are trying to recall a piece of information they are more likely to raise their eyes up and to the left. If they are trying to make something up, they're more likely to look up and to the right.

• Does your friend keep trying to change the subject? She may do this rather obviously – pointing and saying, 'Oooh! Look over there!' – or she may be more subtle, saying 'Did you watch that film last night?' You can play this game, too. Try changing the subject of a conversation quickly yourself – if your pal is a fibber she will be glad and look more relaxed. An innocent person may look confused by your sudden change of topic.

• Avoiding eye contact is a well-known sign that someone is not telling the truth. However, a lot of people know this fact, and someone telling a lie might try to make as much eye contact as possible in order to fool you. So you need to look out for either a lack of eye contact or more eye contact than usual.

Warning: These traits are just guidelines. Just because your friend may behave in a few of the ways described above, it doesn't mean she is lying. Don't let your suspicions lead you to accuse her, as it could hurt her feelings.

HOW TO WRITE 'HAPPY BIRTHDAY' IN TEN DIFFERENT LANGUAGES

With this helpful guide, you'll be a huge hit at any international birthday celebration.

AROUND THE WORLD

Bengali ...   Shubho Jônmodin

Danish ...   Tillykke med fødselsdagen

Dutch ...   Gelukkige verjaardag

Finnish ...   Hyvää syntymäpäivää!

French ...   Joyeux anniversaire

German ...   Alles Gute zum Geburtstag

Hawaiian ...   Hau'oli Lā Hānau

Portuguese ...   Parabéns Feliz aniversário

Italian ...   Buon compleanno

Spanish ...   Feliz cumpleaños

HOW TO READ SOMEONE'S MIND

Most 'mind-readers' use clever techniques and a lot of practice to make it seem as though they can read people's minds. You can do it, too, with this simple mind-reading trick. You're sure to convince an audience of your friends that you can tell what someone is thinking.

You Will Need:

- a magician's hat (or a bowl with high sides)
- paper cut into strips • a pen • an A4 pad

WHAT YOU DO

1. Ask your friends to call out the names of ten celebrities. As the first one is called out, write it down on a slip of paper, fold it up and put it into the hat.

2. When the second name is called out, pretend to write it down on another slip of paper but, instead, write down the first name again. Fold it and put it into the hat.

3. Do the same thing for all the other names – until you have ten slips of paper in the hat, all with the same name on them.

4. Ask one friend to choose a slip of paper from the hat. Tell her that she is not to read it out loud nor let you see it, but to concentrate on the name.

5. Look at her intently and place your hands on either side of your head, as though a mysterious force is at work.

6. After a few moments nod, then write the first famous name on an A4 pad, large enough for your whole audience to read.

7. Ask your friend to reveal the name of the person she picked out of the hat to the audience, as you turn over the A4 pad. They will be amazed.

Warning. Remove the magician's hat quickly before anyone investigates the other slips of paper inside it.

HOW TO HOST YOUR OWN AWARDS CEREMONY

Whether you've done super-well in your exams or if you fancy celebrating your friends' achievements, why not host an awards ceremony, complete with a red carpet?

INVITATIONS AND ENVELOPES

Design some invitations to the ceremony. Use metallic pen to write them – gold lettering on white card looks particularly stylish. The invite should include the date, time and the venue of the ceremony. Make sure the invites are posted out to your pals with plenty of time to spare.

You need to decide on the different categories you are going to present awards for. They need to be suited to your friends' talents and could include – Best Friend in Need, Greenest Friend, Greatest Gift to the Eyeliner Industry, Coolest Geek, Best Karaoke Performance. Make sure everyone invited to the ceremony can win at least one category.

Decorate envelopes for each category. Put the name of the category and the names of three friends who have been nominated for the award on the front. Slip a piece of paper naming the winner inside.

Warn all your guests that they should prepare a dazzling yet tearful acceptance speech, thanking everyone they've ever met in case they win an award. Remind them that they should also practise smiling convincingly and clapping loudly if someone else wins the award they are nominated for.

SETTING THE SCENE

You'll need awards to hand out. These could be cardboard 'Oscars', or certificates you've designed and printed yourself. You could even give out little gifts, such as a chocolate bar, your friend's favourite magazine or a bunch of flowers.

Finally, find a length of cheap, red fabric – scour charity shops for old red curtains or a bright red duvet cover – to act as a red carpet outside the entrance to your house.

AND THE WINNER IS . . .

On the night of the award ceremony, get all your friends to dress up in their best dresses, with as much bling as possible. As they walk up the 'red carpet', get someone in your family to take a few photos – this may be the closest to the paparazzi they ever come. You can choose the best one to give them as a souvenir later.

Hand each friend one category envelope to present at the ceremony – but make sure there's no peaking inside.

Start the proceedings by presenting the first category award yourself. Put on an Oscar-worthy performance to show your mates how it is done and present the award with a flourish.

Choose another member of your family to be in charge of the music. They need to switch it on when someone goes up to receive an award and again when they leave. They must turn it down during acceptance speeches and turn it on full blast if a speech gets dull to encourage that person to leave the stage.

Remember – it's all showbiz!

HOW TO PLAY A COOL CARD GAME

'Noses' is a very simple card game that's bound to make you laugh. You just need a pack of cards and between 4 and 13 players.

Take all four suits (hearts, clubs, diamonds and spades) of any numbered card from the pack – for example all four 2s. Remove one set for each player in the game, so if there are five of you, take all four suits of five numbered cards. Put aside the remaining cards. Shuffle the cards you removed well, and deal them all out so each player has four cards.

Players must sit in a circle. Each person must take a card from her hand and place it face down to her left, and pick up the card that has been placed on her right.

As soon as any player has collected all four suits of the same numbered card, she must casually put a finger on her nose and stop passing cards. If she is the first to do this, she is the winner. Everyone else must signal that they've noticed the end of the game by casually putting their fingers on their noses, too. The last person without a finger on her nose has to pay a forfeit, such as telling a joke, doing a handstand, or dancing the hornpipe – you decide!

HOW TO MAKE A FIZZY DRINK

Make your very own fizz powder and add it to your favourite juice to make a unique drink you've invented yourself.

You Will Need:

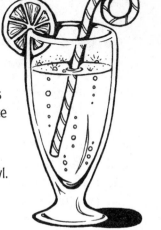

• six teaspoons citric acid monohydrate powder (available from pharmacies) • three teaspoons bicarbonate of soda • two tablespoons of icing sugar • fruit juice of your choice

WHAT YOU DO

Mix the dry ingredients together in a bowl. Put two teaspoons of this powder into a glass and add some fruit juice. Simple!

HOW TO SURVIVE A SHOAL OF PIRANHAS

You might have heard that a shoal of vicious piranha fish can strip a human being to her skeleton in a matter of seconds, but this is just not true.

In reality, these toothy fish don't live up to their fearsome reputation. There are lots of different kinds of piranha fish, and some are actually vegetarians. Even the most dangerous piranhas do not prey on large mammals (like you). It is true, however, that a piranha fish can give you a very nasty nip – in fact it could easily bite off a finger or a toe.

You should be prepared for any situation, especially ones that involve ferocious fish with sharp teeth. Here are some tips on how to hang on to all your digits in piranha-infested waters.

PREVENTIVE MEASURES

- Be aware of piranha habitats – they live in slow-moving rivers, streams and lakes in South America. The most dangerous type is the red-bellied piranha.

- Don't enter any of the large pools that can form beside rivers after heavy rainfall. Piranhas might have become trapped in these pools and, if they have, they will be very hungry indeed, and much more likely to attack.

- The dry season can also be a dangerous time to go into the rivers of South America – piranha prey can be in short supply during this time, so they will be peckish.

- Avoid water close to rubbish dumps, or trees where birds nest – these can be rich sources of food for piranhas, so the fish are more likely to lurk there.

- Piranha fish can sense blood in the water, so don't enter the water if you have a bleeding cut anywhere on your body.

- If you do see piranhas, don't panic – thrashing about will only attract them and other predators. Move calmly and smoothly through the water to the bank, where you can get out and panic in relative safety.

HOW TO MAKE
A STEP-PYRAMID CAKE

This cake makes an ideal centre piece for an Egyptian-themed party – it's simply fit for a pharaoh.

You Will Need:

Important Note. The quantities listed below make one square cake. You will need to make three cakes in order to create your pyramid, so you need to have three times all ingredients listed.

- 200 g butter • 200 g caster sugar • four eggs
- one teaspoon vanilla essence • 200 g self-raising flour
- 100 g plain flour • jam • whipped cream
- icing sugar

WHAT YOU DO

1. Preheat the oven to 160°C/Gas Mark 3, and line and grease your cake tin.

2. Mix the butter and sugar together vigorously with a wooden spoon until it's light and fluffy.

3. Add one egg and stir the mixture thoroughly. Repeat until all four eggs have been added, one by one. Then stir in the vanilla essence.

4. Sift the self-raising and plain flour together in a separate bowl, then gently mix it into the egg, butter and sugar mixture.

5. Pour the mixture into a 20 cm square cake tin lined with baking parchment. Bake it in the centre of the oven for about

75 minutes. You can check the cake is ready by putting a skewer into the middle of the cake – it should come out clean.

Warning. Always wear oven gloves when putting something in the oven or taking it out. Get an adult to help you.

6. Take the cake out of the oven, remove it from the tin and leave it to cool on a wire rack.

7. Make two more cakes like this one, using the same method.

TO MAKE THE PYRAMID

The first cake will form the base of your pyramid. Place it in the centre of a cake board.

For the next layer, trim 4 cm of cake from the length and width of another cake, so that you are left with a cake measuring 16 cm x 16 cm. Spread one side of the square with a layer of jam and carefully stick it in the centre of the first layer.

The final square cake makes several layers. First cut one square which measures 12 cm by 12 cm. Spread one side with jam and place it in the centre of the first two layers.

From the remaining cake, cut another square, measuring 8 cm by 8 cm, and one measuring 4 cm by 4 cm. Spread each square with jam and cream, and place them one after the other on top of your pyramid.

FINISHING TOUCHES

Using a sieve, sprinkle icing sugar all over your pyramid – in Egyptian times, some pyramids were covered in a layer of white limestone which made them glisten in sunlight.

You have made an Egyptian step pyramid! Why not have an Egyptian-themed party and dress up as Cleopatra?

HOW TO MAKE A POP-UP CARD

This flower card is very easy to make and it looks amazing. It's perfect for Mother's Day or a friend's birthday.

You Will Need:

- an A4 sheet of coloured paper • scissors • a glue stick • pens

WHAT YOU DO

1. Fold the paper in half lengthways, then fold the top layer in half again.

2. Cut down the two fold marks you have made and you will have three strips of paper – one wide and two narrow.

3. Take one of the narrow strips and fold it in half so the short ends are together. Then fold it in half twice more, so you have a small rectangle, eight layers thick.

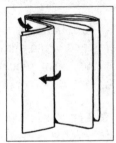

4. Make one final fold, to find the centre of the rectangle, then open it out and round off the top corners with your scissors. Make a small notch in the centre to complete your petal shape.

5. Repeat steps 3 and 4 with the other narrow strip.

6. Make four notches in each strip, as shown here.

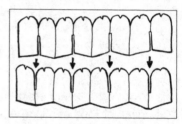

7. Slot them together, so that they weave in and out. Then, starting at one end of the strip, flatten out the pairs of petals so that you end up with eight pairs of petals side by side.

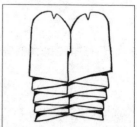

8. Take the wide strip of paper – cut it in half along the width and discard one piece. Fold the remaining piece in half – this is the outside of your pop-up card.

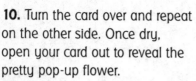

9. Place your petals in the centre of the card and put a dab of glue at each point shown here. Close the card over it and press firmly.

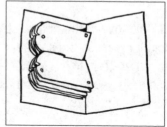

10. Turn the card over and repeat on the other side. Once dry, open your card out to reveal the pretty pop-up flower.

11. Now use felt-tip pens to decorate the front of the card with your greeting – 'Happy Birthday', or 'Happy Mother's Day', for instance.

HOW TO CREATE YOUR OWN LIGHTNING

It's so easy to make your own mini version of lightning – you don't need to create a thunderstorm first. Here's how ...

You Will Need:

• a blown-up balloon • a piece of woollen cloth
• a paperclip

WHAT YOU DO

1. This technique works best when the weather is very dry, so don't bother trying it on a misty, autumn day. Darken the room – the darker it is, the better you'll see your homemade lightning.

2. Rub the balloon against the wool for 30 seconds.

3. Hold the balloon close to the paperclip.

4. You should see a spark crackling between the balloon and the paperclip – just like a mini version of forked lightning. In fact, the static electricity you built up on the surface of the balloon is attracted to the metal of the paperclip.

HOW TO MAKE
A FAKE FOSSIL

It's not difficult to make fake fossils that would be worthy of any palaeontologist's collection. (A palaeontologist is someone who studies fossils.)

You Will Need:

- modelling clay • a rolling pin
- an object to fossilize – small plastic toy insects, animals or dinosaurs, or a shell or bone • a paintbrush
- petroleum jelly • plaster of Paris • water

WHAT YOU DO

1. Knead the modelling clay until it's soft, then roll it out flat with your rolling pin. Roll it out to about 2 cm thick. Make sure it's bigger than the object you want to fossilize.

2. Use the paintbrush to cover the object you want to fossilize with a thin layer of petroleum jelly (this will make it easier to remove from the clay later).

3. Push the object into the clay. Leave it there until the clay is completely dry – 24 hours or so – and then remove it. You now have your fossil mould.

4. To make your cast, you need to make up the plaster of Paris in a plastic container (follow the instructions on the packet).

5. Use your paintbrush to cover the inside of your mould with a thin layer of petroleum jelly.

6. Pour the plaster of Paris into the mould. Leave it to set for at least 30 minutes.

7. Remove the cast and leave it to dry completely.

You now have a cool fake fossil. Why not create a whole collection of prehistoric bugs, bones and mini-dinosaurs?

HOW TO MAKE YOUR OWN PAPER

If you have any sheets of waste paper for recycling, why not have a go at making your own paper with it? Handmade paper will make a great greetings card or notelet.

You Will Need:

- wastepaper (any kind will do, coloured or white – tissue paper, printer paper, wrapping paper, etc, but not newspaper)
- a mixing bowl • water • a blender
- a large washing-up bowl • a wire coat hanger
- a pair of nylon tights (the kind you can see through)
- lots of newspaper

WHAT YOU DO

1. Tear your waste paper into small pieces and soak it in a bowl of water until it is soft.

2. Transfer the soaked paper into a blender and top up with water. Blend the mixture until there are no large pieces of paper left. Your mixture should be a thick pulp, like porridge, so use a bit of trial and error to get the right mixture of paper to water.

3. Fill the washing-up bowl with about four times as much water as you have pulp. Stir the pulp into the water in the washing-up bowl. At this point you can include some extra bits and pieces to make your paper individual. Here are some ideas:

- glitter - dried flower petals - pieces of coloured thread
- leaves - seeds - food colouring

4. Bend the coat hanger into a rectangle – this wire frame will be the shape of your finished sheet of paper. (Get an adult to help with this bit as the hanger may have sharp ends.)

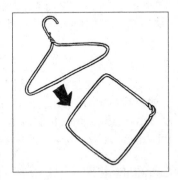

5. Stretch one leg of the tights over your wire frame and tie the ends either side (these will act as your handles).

6. Lower your wire frame into the washing-up bowl, keeping it as flat as possible. Then carefully lift it out again, covered in pulp.

7. Lay the frame on some newspaper to thoroughly dry out – you can speed up the process by leaving it in a warm place such as an airing cupboard.

8. Once it's dry, gently peel the paper off the frame.

Experiment with different types of paper, colours and added bits and pieces, for the best results.

HOW TO PLAY 'TRUTH OR DARE' . . . AND SURVIVE

'Truth or Dare' is a great sleepover game for two or more players – as long as you keep well away from dangerous dares and upsetting truths! Here's how to play and some suggestions for 'truths' and 'dares'.

WHAT YOU DO

Before the game starts, write some truths and dares on slips of paper (see opposite for inspiration). Fold them up and put the truths in one pile and the dares in another.

Gather the players together, sitting in a circle. The youngest person in the circle starts – becoming the 'Questioner'. She selects another player to be the 'Answerer', and asks her, 'Truth or dare?' The Answerer chooses which type of question she would like to answer. The questioner picks a slip of paper from the appropriate pile and reads it out. The Answerer deals with the consequences as best she can!

Here are some ideas – make up some more of your own, but be sure to stay away from anything dangerous, gross or upsetting! Remember, you have to answer truthfully...

TRUTHS

What is your favourite daydream?

Who would like to be marooned on a desert island with?

Who would you least like to be marooned on a desert island with?

Have you ever had a crush on a friend's brother?

When and where were you happiest?

What's the stupidest answer you've ever given to a teacher's question?

Describe your ideal sixteenth birthday party.

If you won £1 million, what would you do with it?

What's your dream holiday?

If the world was going to end tomorrow, what would you do today?

DARES

Put two ice cubes inside your T-shirt.

Do a cartwheel.

Eat a teaspoonful of mustard.

Do an impression of your least favourite teacher.

Swap an article of clothing with the person on your right.

Sing 'I'm a Little Teapot' and do all the actions.

Go outside and sing 'Baa, Baa, Black Sheep' loudly.

Wear a pair of socks on your hands, and keep them on for the rest of the game.

Hum the national anthem without laughing.

Give the person on your left a piggyback around the room.

HOW TO BLING UP YOUR BAG

Use your design skills to give a boring bag some super style.

HEART FELT

You'll love these gorgeous hearts ...

You Will Need:

- a pencil • several sheets of white paper
- sheets of coloured craft foam or felt
- scissors • PVA glue • fake jewels
- self-adhesive hook-and-loop tape

WHAT YOU DO

1. Draw a selection of heart shapes in different sizes on a sheet of paper – you can trace over the ones shown here. Cut them out.

2. Draw around your paper templates on the foam or felt. Use several contrasting colours. Cut out the shapes.

3. Dab some glue in the middle of the largest heart and stick the next largest heart on to it. Keep going until you've used them all. Why not add a fake jewel on the final layer?

4. Fix a square of hook-and-loop tape to your bag, and another to the back of your heart – then press the bag and the heart together.

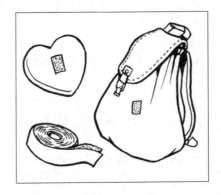

Top Tip. Try using different designs: stars, flowers or animal shapes, for example.

HOW TO MAKE UP A ROPE ROUTINE

Skipping is a great way to keep fit, and it's fun, too. Master these complex routines and wow your friends.

SKIPPING MOVES

First practise these basic moves:

- **Backwards Jump:** just turn the rope backwards instead of forwards.

- **Double Jump:** jump up high and turn the rope twice before you land.

- **Hop-And-Skip Jump:** land on your right foot, then on your left.

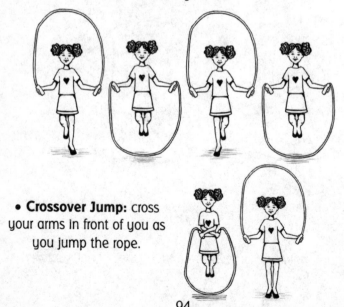

- **Crossover Jump:** cross your arms in front of you as you jump the rope.

- **Slalom:** land with your knees to the right, then with your knees to the left – as if you were skiing down a slalom slope.

- **Jumping Jill:** land with your feet apart, then with your feet together.

- **Figure-Of-Eight Jump:** move the rope in a figure of eight pattern while you stand still.

- **Balanced Jump:** put your right hand under your right knee as you turn the rope – carry on skipping and land on your left leg. Then put your left hand under your left knee and land on your right leg.

ROUTINES

Once you have mastered these basic moves, try putting them together in this routine:

5 double jumps; 5 backwards jumps; 10 hop-and-skip jumps; 5 figure-of-eight jumps; 2 crossover jumps; 5 jumping Jills; 2 balanced jumps.

Why not make up some jumps and routines of your own?

HOW TO COUNT IN ROMAN NUMERALS

The Romans were good at lots of things, but they had a very awkward number system. If you were an ancient Roman, this is what you could have had to contend with:

I (unus) = 1
V (quinque) = 5
X (decem) = 10
L (quinquaginta) = 50
C (centum) = 100
D (quingenti) = 500
M (mille) = 1,000

All the numbers in between are written with these numerals, too. For example, numbers 1, 2 and 3 are I, II and III.

If there's a smaller numeral in front of a larger one, this means you subtract the smaller number from the larger one. So:

$$IV = 5 \text{ minus } 1 = 4$$
$$IX = 10 \text{ minus } 1 = 9$$
$$XL = 50 \text{ minus } 10 = 40$$
$$VC = 100 \text{ minus } 5 = 95$$

A larger numeral followed by a smaller one means you should add the numbers together. For example:

$$VII = 5 \text{ plus } 2 = 7$$
$$XVI = 10 \text{ plus } 5 \text{ plus } 1 = 16$$
$$LX = 50 \text{ plus } 10 = 60$$
$$CLV = 100 \text{ plus } 50 \text{ plus } 5 = 155$$

Bigger numbers can be shown by adding a line on top of a numeral, which multiplies it by 1,000. For example:

$$\overline{V} = 5,000$$
$$\overline{L} = 50,000$$
$$\overline{C} = 100,000$$
$$\overline{M} = 1,000,000$$

If you think all this is confusing, try multiplication and long division using Roman numerals!

HOW TO SURVIVE A RIP CURRENT

A rip current is an area of water near the surface of the sea that is flowing rapidly away from shore. Rip currents can pull even the strongest swimmers out to sea. However, once you know how to deal with rip currents, you should be able to get back to shore safely.

EMERGENCY TACTICS

If you are swimming and suddenly realize you are being pulled out to sea by a current, don't panic! Panicking will only make you disoriented – you need to keep a clear head. You have a very good chance of getting back to shore, and the current won't drag you under the water.

Don't try and swim back to shore. You won't be strong enough to swim against the current, and trying to do so will

just tire you out. Swim parallel with the line of the beach. If the pull of the current makes this too difficult, just wait until the current takes you into an area of calmer water.

Rip currents are usually no more than about ten metres wide. Once you've swum far enough along, parallel to the beach, you should arrive outside the area affected by the current. Then you should be able to swim back in to shore, or you can let the waves take you back in.

On tourist beaches there are usually signs warning you if the area is prone to dangerous rip currents. Take notice of these warnings and never swim in areas that are marked as unsafe. Always stick to the area of the beach that is patrolled by a trained lifeguard.

Warning. Don't go into the sea on your own, and if you're not a strong swimmer, stay in shallow water.

HOW TO MEASURE A TREE

You don't need to climb to the top branches trailing a very long tape measure to calculate the height of a tree. Here's an easy method that involves no scrambling through leaves.

You Will Need:

• a brightly coloured ribbon • a tape measure
• a pencil • oh, and a tree

WHAT YOU DO

1. With the tape measure, affix your ribbon around the trunk at a point 1.5 metres from the base of the tree.

2. Walk away from the tree until you can see the whole tree and the marker. Hold your pencil upright at arm's length, and close one eye. Line up the bottom of the tree with the bottom of your pencil, and move your thumb nail up the pencil until it lines up with the marker on the trunk. The distance you have measured along your pencil is equivalent to 1.5 metres.

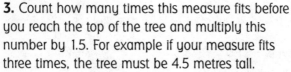

3. Count how many times this measure fits before you reach the top of the tree and multiply this number by 1.5. For example if your measure fits three times, the tree must be 4.5 metres tall.

HOW TO BUILD A GINGERBREAD HOUSE

Building your own gingerbread house takes time, but the result will be worth it. And it tastes as good as it looks!

You Will Need:

(To make the house template)
• thick paper or card • a pencil • scissors

(To make the gingerbread)
• 250 g unsalted butter • 200 g brown sugar
• seven tablespoons of golden syrup • 600 g plain flour
• two teaspoons of baking powder • five teaspoons of ground ginger

(To decorate your house)
• 500 g icing sugar • small pack of marzipan
• coloured sweets • chocolate buttons
• edible silver balls and other cake decorations

WHAT YOU DO

1. Draw each of the three shapes shown on page 102 on a sheet of thick paper or card at the sizes specified. Cut them out.

2. Heat the oven to 200°C/Gas Mark 6. Melt the butter, sugar and syrup together in a saucepan.

3. In a big bowl, mix together the flour, baking powder and ginger. Then stir in the mixture from the saucepan to make your gingerbread dough.

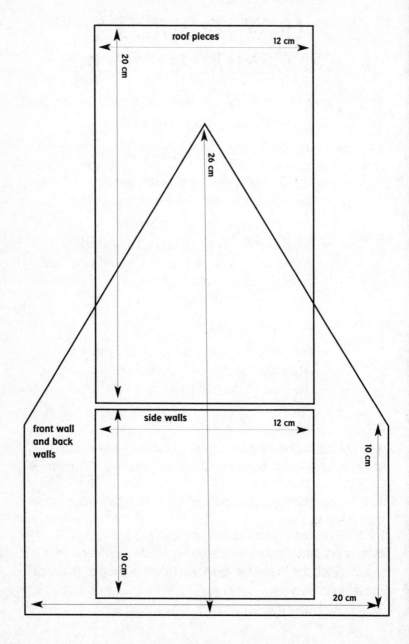

4. Take about a quarter of the dough and roll it out on a lightly floured piece of baking parchment, until it's 0.5 cm thick. Place the template of one of the front walls on top of the dough and cut around it with a knife. Place this shape, still on its baking parchment, on to a baking tray.

5. Put the trimmings back with the rest of the dough, squash it all into a ball and then roll some more out on another piece of baking parchment to 0.5 cm. Continue until you have two of each shape on the baking trays. The shapes will grow while cooking, so leave plenty of space between them.

6. Bake your gingerbread shapes in the oven for between 10 and 15 minutes – until the dough is golden and darker at the edges. Take them out of the oven and leave to cool completely. (Get an adult to help with the oven.)

7. Use your left-over dough to make trees and flowers for the garden of your house, or little gingerbread people to 'live' in it.

8. Make up some icing according to the packet instructions. This will glue your house together.

9. Once cooled, take your wall shapes and spread the icing over the edges. Join them together, piece by piece – you might need a friend to help you with this bit. Support your walls with books, mugs or tins of food and leave them to dry for a couple of hours. Then put the roof on in the same way.

10. Now decorate your house in any way you like. You could use a piece of marzipan for the door – perhaps with a chocolate button door knob and edible silver balls for the door frame. You could use icing for the roof (or just dust it with icing sugar). Stick your sweets onto the house with icing.

Can you bear to eat the gingerbread house? It'll keep for about a week while you make up your mind.

HOW TO SKIM STONES

Making a stone bounce across the surface of a lake or river takes skill. With a bit of practice you might even be able to beat the current world record of 51 bounces ...

Choose a flat, oval-shaped stone that fits easily inside your palm and find an area of calm water, such as a lake or pond.

Stand side-on to the water and crouch with your feet apart.

Curl your index finger around the edge of the stone and place your thumb flat on top of it. Your middle finger should be underneath, making sure the stone stays horizontal when you throw it.

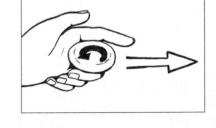

Draw back your arm and then jerk it forward, using your wrist and index finger to spin the stone as it leaves your hand. You need to throw the stone as near to the surface of the water as you can, and almost parallel to it. If you want to be technical, you're aiming for an angle of around 20° between the path of the stone and the surface of the water.

The front of the stone should be a little higher than the back to give it a better chance of bouncing.

HOW TO MAKE A PHOTO FRAME

If you have a photograph you love, why not create a special frame for it?

You Will Need:

• two pieces of thick card (old cardboard boxes are good)
• a pencil • a ruler • scissors • newspaper • a mixture of
100 ml water and 100 ml PVA glue • a paintbrush • extra
glue • poster paint • decorations, such as fake jewels, shells,
sweets, cake decorations or dried flowers • a sheet of clear
acetate (available from stationers) • sticky tape

WHAT YOU DO

1. Place the photo you want to frame on a piece of card and draw around it. Draw another square inside the first one, about half a centimetre narrower on each side.

106

2. Draw another square outside the first two, making sure the first two squares are right in the middle. This will be the part of the frame you see, so make it as big as you like.

3. Cut out the smallest and the largest square.

You should be left with a frame of cardboard. (Ask an adult to help with cutting out the centre, as this can be a bit tricky.)

4. On another piece of card, draw around the outside of your frame. Cut the square out to form the back of your frame.

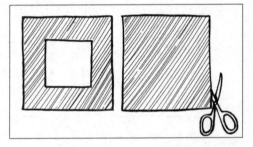

5. To give your frame some depth, tear a newspaper into strips, and dip the pieces in the PVA-glue-and-water mixture. Cover the frame with them. Wait until they dry, then add another layer of strips. Repeat until you have added four layers.

6. When your final layer of newspaper is completely dry, paint over it with the diluted glue and leave it to dry overnight.

7. Now paint your photo frame.

8. Arrange your chosen decorations on the frame, then glue them into place. Choose decorations to suit the subject of the photo. When they are stuck in place, cover with undiluted PVA glue to seal them and make them shine.

9. Cut a square out of the sheet of clear acetate at least one centimetre larger on each side than the window in your frame. Make a crease in the bottom edge of the acetate (for your photo to sit in), then use sticky tape to secure it on the reverse side of the frame with the bottom flap sticking out.

10. Attach the back of your frame to the reverse of the front, gluing it on three sides, leaving the top side of the frame open.

11. Slip your photo into the frame and position it in the window.

HOW TO MAKE FRIENDS WITH A YETI

The Yeti is also known as the Abominable Snowman. Does the word 'abominable' worry you at all? Perhaps it should – especially bearing in mind that a Yeti is said to be three metres tall and weigh about 600 kg. However, if you're quite sure you want to be best mates with a large, hairy, mythical creature, here's some advice:

• First, find your Yeti. This will not be easy. You need to travel to the Himalayan mountains of Nepal and Tibet. You will need to bring plenty of warm clothes – the Yeti has thick fur to keep him warm. There are reports of similar creatures in other mountains of the world – you could try the Sasquatch in Canada, Bigfoot in America, Mapinguary in Brazil or Yowie in Australia.

• The Yeti is rarely seen, so it must be very shy. Don't make any sudden movements, and try to look friendly and

approachable. Be patient – it may be a long time before the Yeti decides you are friendly.

• A Yeti is very hairy, so it may not be a good companion for you if you suffer from pet allergies – sudden sneezing may alarm it.

• Try tempting out your Yeti with food. Reports agree that the Yeti is an ape-like creature, so imagine what an ape might like to eat.

• Once you have charmed your Yeti, try interesting it in winter sports such as snowboarding, skiing or sledging. It may already be an expert, in which case it could teach you some impressive tricks.

• Speaking to your Yeti could be a problem: it may not speak English. In fact, it might be able to communicate only in chimp-like grunts and shrieks. You'll have to find other fun things to do together to make up for the lack of conversation. As well as winter sports, try toasting marshmallows over a campfire, star-gazing or flying kites.

HOW TO MAKE
AN ORIGAMI BOX

These little boxes are very cute, as well as being useful for storing paperclips, beads, craft supplies or sweets. They're really easy to make, though you'll find it more difficult with thicker card. All you need is a square piece of paper.

WHAT YOU DO

1. Fold the paper in half, then open it out and fold it in half the other way. Every time you fold the paper, make a sharp crease.

2. Open the paper out again and fold it in half diagonally. Open it out and fold it in half diagonally the other way.

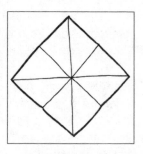

3. Open the paper out and fold all four corners into the centre.

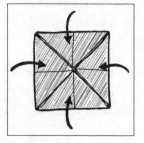

4. Fold two opposite sides into the centre. Open them out again, then fold the other two sides into the centre in the same way, and open out again. These will be the sides of your box.

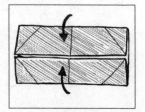

5. Open out two opposite corners, as shown. Push the point at the edge of one of the sides inwards, so that you're reversing the fold. Do the same with the other side.

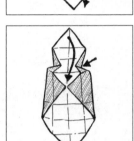

6. Now bring the point of the flap over, and tuck it around the two reversed folds to make the third side of the box.

7. Repeat steps 5 and 6 to make the fourth side.

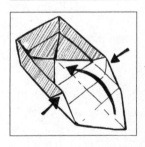

8. To make a lid for your box, repeat steps 1 to 6 with a square of paper, half a centimetre larger than the first in length and width.

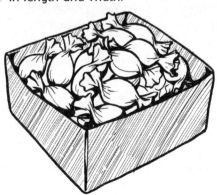

Top Tip. This is a great way of recycling greetings cards. Make your lid out of the front cover and use the back of the card for the bottom of the box.

HOW TO BECOME A FAMOUS ACTRESS

Do you dream of fans adoring you, of travelling by private jet, and seeing giant posters of yourself all over the place? Follow the tips below and a life of superstardom may be yours:

- Pay extra attention in drama lessons. Take an acting course outside school as well, if possible.

- Practise as much as you can and take part in school productions and local theatre groups – you need talent, but experience helps.

- To start off your career, try to get work as an 'extra' – these are people with non-speaking roles who appear in the background of movies and TV dramas. Be prepared to take whatever roles are offered.

- Never turn down a party invitation: you never know who you might meet – a talent-spotter or a famous director.

- Get a professional photograph taken of your head and shoulders (known in the business as a 'headshot'). List all your acting experience on the back. If you have other talents and abilities, such as singing, parachuting, ice-skating, martial arts or Irish dancing, list them, too – they might be just what a director is looking for. Don't list anything you really can't do in case you are asked to prove it.

- You'll need an agent to help you land big roles and handle all the financial and legal negotiations that go on in the film

business. Send copies of your headshots to as many agents as possible.

- Move to a big city. If you've set your heart on being a star in Hollywood, this will have to be Los Angeles.

- Practise looking glamorous, and get a friend to pretend to be your assistant – she should constantly shout into a mobile phone and carry lots of papers that look like film scripts.

- Contacts are vital. Maintain good relationships with directors, agents and fellow actors by being polite, punctual and professional at all times.

- Develop a thick skin. When you're in the limelight you'll receive lots of flattery and lots of criticism. Try to ignore both, unless they come from someone whose opinion you trust.

HOW TO KNOW YOUR BIRTH-MONTH FLOWER

There's a special flower (or sometimes two) for every month of the year. If it's the birthday of someone you care about, why not give her a bunch of her birth-month flowers? You could attach a card explaining what the flowers symbolize.

MONTH	FLOWER	MEANING
January	Carnation or snowdrop	Love or friendship in hard times
February	Violet or primrose	Faithfulness or love
March	Daffodil	Devotion
April	Daisy or sweetpea	Innocence or goodbye
May	Lily-of-the-valley or hawthorn	Sweetness or hope
June	Rose or honeysuckle	Love
July	Larkspur	Laughter
August	Gladiola	Sincerity
September	Aster	Love
October	Calendula	Happiness
November	Chrysanthemum	Happiness and wealth
December	Poinsettia	Good wishes for the future

HOW TO READ TEA LEAVES

Some people claim to be able to see the future in the pattern of tea leaves left in a cup. Today, most people use teabags to make a cup of tea, but buy some loose leaf tea or cut open a tea bag, and have a go at predicting your own future.

BREWING UP THE FUTURE

1. Select a white cup to make your tea in – this will make it easier to see the tea leaves left over.

2. Brew your tea with the loose leaves, but don't use a tea strainer. Drink it, leaving only a little in the bottom of the cup.

3. Hold the cup in your left hand and swirl it around three times in a clockwise direction. Turn the cup upside down on a saucer to drain away the liquid. After seven seconds, turn the cup the right way up again.

4. Now turn the cup so the handle is pointing towards you. Look inside – what patterns do you see? A bird could mean freedom, and a shoe that you're about to go on a long journey.

Don't expect your predictions to come true every time. Maybe all you'll see are soggy tea leaves.

HOW TO AVOID A SHARK ATTACK

You are very unlikely to be attacked by a shark. But even if the chances of being bitten by a huge, ferocious predator are very remote indeed, it's a good idea to reduce the risk as much as you possibly can. Being eaten alive ruins any trip to the seaside.

• You could eliminate the risk of a shark attack completely by not swimming in the sea at all. Failing that, you could stay out of the sea in shark-attack hotspots, such as the eastern United States (especially Florida), which has more shark attacks than any other part of the world.

- Listen out for warnings on the radio or TV of shark sightings in the area you are staying.

- Don't swim in the sea on your own, as sharks are more likely to attack lone swimmers than a group of bathers.

- Your swimsuit could attract a shark if it's brightly coloured or has strong, contrasting colours – sharks can't see very well, so they're likely to take an interest in anything that stands out. Don't wear jewellery or anything shiny, as a shark could mistake it for fish scales flashing in the water.

- Avoid lots of splashing about, which can interest a shark because it could be a creature in distress.

- Don't go swimming at dawn and dusk, or at night – sharks are likely to feed at those times.

- Sharks often lurk near sandbars and steep drop-offs: stay away from them, or be on the look-out for a fin slicing through the water towards you.

- Sharks are well known for their ability to detect blood in the water from kilometres away. Don't go swimming in the sea if you have an open cut anywhere on your body.

- Sharks feed on smaller fish and marine mammals. Don't go swimming in areas where there are likely to be lots of these 'bait' creatures – you could find yourself in the middle of a shark snack bar. Diving sea birds are a sign that there are plenty of bait fish in the sea. If you see people fishing it is a sure sign that bait creatures are around.

HOW TO DUST FOR FINGERPRINTS

Do you need to carry out your own crime-scene investigation? Dusting for prints could reveal who's been at the biscuit jar, or who sneaked a peek at your top-secret diary.

You Will Need:

- some fine powder (talcum powder or cocoa powder work well) • a paintbrush • some clear sticky tape • a piece of card

LIFTING PRINTS

1. Taking an imprint of fingerprints using the technique described below is known as 'lifting' prints. Finger prints are hard to lift from a grainy surface like wood, so look for some that have been left on a smooth, shiny surface, such as a mirror or a glass.

2. Very gently, and as evenly as possible, brush some powder over the surface of the prints with your paintbrush. Blow away any excess.

3. If you have revealed several fingerprints, choose the clearest one. Cut a length of sticky tape and cover the print with it, sticky

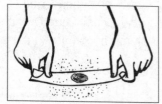

118

side down. Smooth the tape down all over the print area, before carefully lifting it up with the print underneath.

4. Stick the tape containing your print onto some card. If you've used cocoa powder, choose white card. If you've used talc, choose a dark-coloured card.

SELECTING SUSPECTS

Now you need to work out whose fingerprint you have lifted. This will mean taking prints from all of your suspects. You'll need an inked stamp pad and some white paper.

Have a suspect gently roll each of his or her fingertips on the stamp pad, then roll the inky fingertips onto some white paper. If you gently hold the tip of each finger down while it is rolling, this will make the print less likely to smudge.

When you have fingerprinted everyone capable of the crime, use a magnifying glass to compare their fingerprints to the one you have lifted. Can you discover a perfect match and catch the culprit?

HOW TO PLAY 'WHAT'S IN THE BAG?'

'What's In The Bag' is a ghoulish game, perfect to play at a Halloween party or a spoooooky sleepover. Any number of people can play.

Shortly before your guests arrive, gather a selection of opaque polythene bags (which means bags that you can't see through), and a small quantity of each of the following items: peeled raw carrots, peeled grapes, cooked spaghetti, mashed banana, cottage cheese and cooked rice. Put each item into a separate bag.

It's a good idea to play this game at the beginning of your party, because your gross ingredients are best when fresh. As soon as your guests arrive, get them to gather round. Set the scene with a scary story. Tell them that, earlier on, you were passing a graveyard, when you noticed a strange-looking woman sitting in front of a huge cooking pot. She was muttering and throwing things into the pot. You asked her what ingredients she was using and she demanded that you guess by feeling them, not seeing them.

Tell your friends that you have bags containing each of the witch's horrible ingredients. Now it is their turn to identify what they are. Pass around the bags of different ingredients. Tell your friends to feel inside, but not to look.

They probably won't guess what is inside each bag so tell them these chilling ingredients:

- Fingers (carrots) • Eyeballs (grapes) • Maggots (rice)
- Worms (spaghetti) • Bats' brains (cottage cheese)
- Frogs' innards (mashed banana)

HOW TO BUILD A HOUSE OF CARDS

Are you looking for something to while away a rainy afternoon? Do you have lots of patience and a steady hand? Why not build a house of cards? All you need is a deck of playing cards and a draft-free bedroom.

MASTER BUILDER

1. Find a flat surface that isn't too slippery – a short-pile carpet is ideal. Grab an old pack of cards – brand new cards, which are shiny and slippery, are far more difficult to use for a house of cards than old ones.

2. Lean two cards against one another – shortest ends at the top and bottom – to make an upside-down 'V', that looks like a tent. They should be about the same width apart at the bottom as your middle three fingers. This forms the basis of the whole house of cards.

3. Place another tent shape right beside the first one.

4. Place a playing card horizontally across the top of the two tent shapes, to form the floor of your house's second storey.

5. To complete a very small house put another tent shape on top. However, girls who like to be the best at everything probably want to make a bigger, far more impressive house of cards. To do this, you'll need to add three more storeys to create the classic house of cards shown here.

You will need plenty of patience. Don't expect to be a master builder the first time you try.

Warning. No self-respecting builder of card houses would cheat. The cards should stand up because of your amazing balancing skills and not because they've been stuck together with sticky tape!

HOW TO MAKE BUTTERFLY CAKES

These little cakes are simple to make, tasty, pretty and perfect for a birthday party or a sleepover.

You Will Need:

(For the cakes)
- 100 g butter • 100 g caster sugar • two eggs
- 100 g self-raising flour • a teaspoon of vanilla essence
- a dozen cake cases

(For the icing)
- 50 g butter • 100 g icing sugar

(Optional extras)
- hundreds and thousands • small sweets
- crystalized flower petals
- edible silver balls
- food-colouring

WHAT YOU DO

1. Preheat the oven to 190°C/Gas Mark 5.

2. Cream the butter and sugar together (this means beating it with the back of a wooden spoon), until it's light in colour and fluffy. You will need plenty of elbow grease.

3. Beat the eggs together in a separate bowl, then gently stir them into the butter and sugar mixture, a little bit at a time.

4. Sift your flour a little at a time in to the mixture, stirring it in thoroughly each time. Make sure you do this gradually.

5. Add the vanilla essence and stir this in.

6. Place your paper cases in the dips of a cup-cake tin.

7. Spoon the mixture in to the paper cases, filling them half full. You should have enough mixture to make a dozen cakes.

8. Bake for 15 to 20 minutes, until the cakes look golden. (Ask an adult to help you when using the oven.)

9. When they are cool enough to touch, lift your cakes out of the cup-cake tin. Leave them to cool completely on a wire rack.

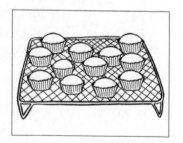

10. Ask an adult to cut a circular section off the top of each cake with a sharp knife. Then cut the circles in half.

11. To prepare some icing, mix the butter and icing sugar together. Spread this on top of each cake in the hollow left by the circle you removed. Then push two halves of the top of the cake into the butter icing, rounded sides facing outwards, so they look like a pair of butterfly wings.

12. Decorate your butterfly cakes with any of the delicious optional extras you gathered. Gorgeous!

Top Tip. Why not add a drop or two of food colouring to the butter icing to introduce a splash of colour to your butterfly cakes?

HOW TO DECORATE YOUR NAILS

Every girl needs tantalizing talons. Here's how to wow with cool, customized nails for a very special occasion.

You Will Need:

- a bowl of warm, soapy water • a nail brush • nail clippers
  • a nail file • cotton buds • nail varnish remover
- cotton wool balls • a cocktail stick • nail varnish in various colours including clear

WHAT YOU DO

1. Submerge your fingers in soapy water for ten minutes to clean the nails and soften your cuticles (the fine layer of skin that grows from the base of the nail). Gently brush the nails with a nail brush, then dry them thoroughly.

2. Trim each of your nails to the same length with nail clippers, then use a nail file to remove sharp edges. Make each nail a similar shape – choose between squares or ovals or 'squovals' (which means a straight top but rounded edges). After filing, give your nails a quick rinse and dry them again.

3. Now choose a bright colour of nail varnish – ruby red or fuchsia pink work well. Roll the bottle of varnish between your palms to warm it up – this makes the varnish easier to apply.

4. Load the brush with a small amount of varnish, taking care to wipe off any excess on the inside of the bottle. Paint a stroke of colour down the middle of your nail first, then down each side to complete it. Practice makes perfect, but remember that the fewer strokes you use the better. Have some nail varnish remover and a cotton bud at the ready to remove minor mistakes.

5. When the first layer is completely dry, apply a second layer of varnish.

6. When this second coat is dry, take the cocktail stick and dip it in some nail varnish that is a pale colour to contrast with the varnish already painted on your nails – white or pale pink work well. Draw a simple design, such as a tiny flower formed from seven dots, or a simple heart – there are some other design suggestions shown below. You need a very steady hand for this, and plenty of practice (you could practise on paper before you try your design on your nails). Reload your cocktail stick with varnish regularly.

7. When your nails are completely dry, apply a top coat of clear varnish to seal in your design.

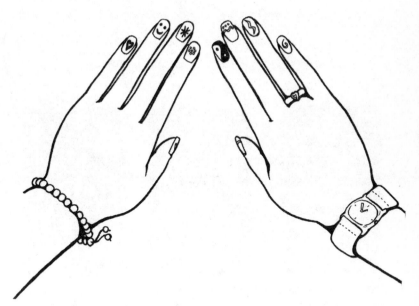

Top Tip. To make your nail varnish dry faster, plunge your fingers into a bowl of ice water (this will NOT work under a running tap) or use a hairdryer on its coolest setting to speed things up.

ALSO AVAILABLE...

The Girls' Book 1:
How To Be The Best
At Everything

ISBN: 978-1-905158-79-9

The Girls' Book 2:
How To Be The Best
At Everything Again

ISBN: 978-1-906082-33-8

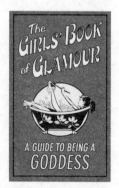

The Girls' Book Of Glamour:
A Guide To Being
A Goddess

ISBN: 978-1-906082-13-0

The Girls' Book Of Secrets:
Shhh... Don't Tell!

ISBN: 978-1-906082-38-3

The Fabulous Girls' Book:
Discover The Secret
Of Being Fabulous

ISBN: 978-1-906082-52-9